EARTH | HEART

the earth gives you a home | the heart gives you significance

warren grossman ph d

 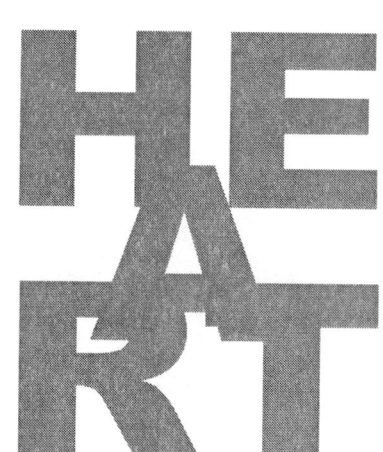

Copyright © 2009 by Warren Grossman Ph D.

Library of Congress Control Number: 2009900672
ISBN: Hardcover 978-1-4415-0614-6
Softcover 978-1-4415-0613-9

All rights reserved. No part of this book may be reproduced or transmitted in any form or by any means, electronic or mechanical, including photocopying, recording, or by any information storage and retrieval system, without permission in writing from the copyright owner.

This book was printed in the United States of America.

To order additional copies of this book, contact:
Xlibris Corporation
1-888-795-4274
www.Xlibris.com
Orders@Xlibris.com

Warren Grossman ph d
18675 parkland dr • 509
shaker heights oh 44122
warren@
warrengrossman.com

HOW

Twenty years ago, I became seriously ill. I remember little of the next six months. When I arose, weak and sick, a life of meaning began.

I then spent countless days lying on the ground instead of the bed, paying careful attention to the meeting place of my body and the earth. This was the way in which I learned about the living surface upon which we exist. There was clearly an exchange of energy between my body and the earth. I became healthy.

At age forty-seven I had become student of nature. I became sensitive to the flow of life in all things. I was surrounded by these teachers, these models of natural existence, such as soil, plants, and trees.

I went to class with my mentors every day. I imitated them attentively. I was changing.

Upon becoming healthy, I did not return to my profession, psychology. I could better represent the simple truths of nature. Most of the time I do this as a healer. A good healer succeeds by, "being nature".

In this book I have done my work with words.

Here are a few words, about what I have learned, and how the unequivocal reality of nature demonstrates not only health, but fine interpersonal behavior.

Warren Grosssman, Ph.D.

2009

WHY

I am a healer.

Healing is done with
the energies
of nature and love.
They are ours to use
for the benefit of others,
although this is not recognized
by our culture.

As I continuously refine this process,
as I listen to my clients,
the same truths are repeatedly evident.

I pay attention to these axioms,
these "natural ethics",
which inhere in nature,
and in the human heart.
This is not lofty rhetoric.

These precepts are
not invented,
or imagined,
or intellectual.
They are real.

I put them into words,
while indulging myself
with the beauty of type.

Warren Grossman, Ph. D

2009

NOT A TABLE OF CONTENTS

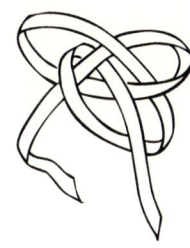

A table of contents lists the parts of a book and the order in which they appear. In this book the pages stand alone, as if they were posters.

Nevertheless, this book has a group of themes:

- ☐ Love—not romance
- ☐ Tolerance—which does not mean to tolerate
- ☐ Interdependence—with the rest of nature
- ☐ Intelligence—not intellect
- ☐ Healing—becoming more whole
- ☐ Forgiving—exchanging anger for love
- ☐ Respect—appreciative regard for that which is not familiar
- ☐ Here and Now—The only time that is neither memory nor fantasy
- ☐ Nature—what you are
- ☐ Transformation—becoming better
- ☐ Epistemology—knowing about knowing

HEALTH IS CONSISTENCY WITH NATURE

Information is not
- *fact*
- *probability*
- *reality*
- *conclusion*

& . it certainly is not experience

The healer provides missing understanding, not missing information

For information go to the internet, media, phone book.

Knowing deeply comes from paying close attention to your life — and life flowing through others.

Understanding arises from mindful intimacy with life.

Ordinary
does not exist

an unconscious
perceptual device
to avoid
continual awe

inform
transform

we can know in different ways
we can be *changed* by experience

Science is a theory about knowing. One creates a hypothesis, gathers data in quantitative form, and transforms the data to support or reject the hypothesis. It can be elegant and sometimes helpful. There are also other ways of knowing.

information • transformation

information ≠ *transformation*

•information

•*transformation*

1

2

THIS IS THE EARTH YOU ARE HOME

POLLUTE THE EARTH YOU ARE HOMELESS

Healing occurs from love in the present.

Attention reduces resistance to possibility. ❖

pay attention

▼ The two internal psoas muscles form a "dynamic keystone" for a strong, balanced body. There is one psoas on either side of the spine. They originate at the transverse processes of the lumbar vertebrae, pass through the pelvis, go over the rim of the thigh joint and attach to the inner side of each femur.

love is my psoas ▲

The psoas is at your body's deepest core. It connects your upper half to your lower half, and your front to your back.

What is less commonly known is that two energy pathways from the heart pass through these two internal muscles.

The psoas muscles are the center of your physical, emotional and spiritual possibilities.

The energy of the heart, which passes through them, makes love, kindness and gentleness possible.

THE PURPOSE OF ANGER IS TO SAVE YOUR LIFE

---

little more

experience
this moment

it to precipitate
it transformation

pay attention

The earth is your mother. She feeds you, even if you are poorly behaved.

Earth lives.

E

it's maternity basis of reality.

MOTHER
Earth

TECHNOLOGY
WONDERFUL | TERRIBLE
?

Why forgive?

To get past your own

past.

Love Heals

Love brings Hope

Love causes Gentleness

Love is Optimistic

Love Forgives

Love is Free

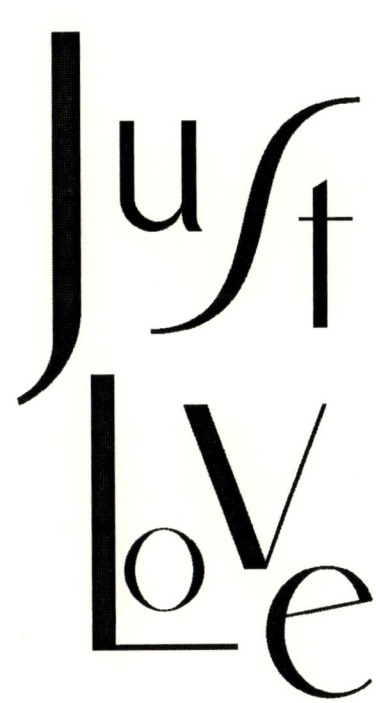

Humility
You are you
You are not more
You are not less

≤ ≥

demeaning yourself is not humility

IF YOU DO NOT

TINY BOXES CALLED "INDOORS" OBSCURE OUR EXPERIENCE OF REALITY | perceive nature as your home

you cannot

feel at home

Connect with nature
love &
forgive — if
not
fall
prey
to
diseases
of
your
own
invention

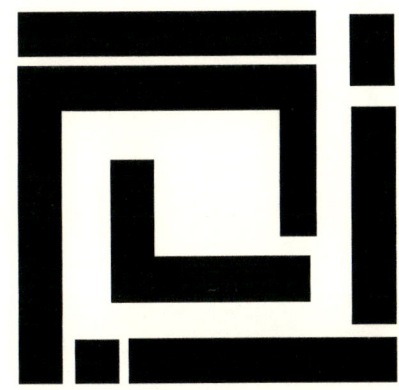

YOU CAN KNOW YOUR EXPERIENCE

OR RECITE OTHER'S WORDS

healer
warren grossman ph d
28675 parkland dr #500
shaker heights oh 44122
216 491 8887
warren@
warrengrossman.com

pay Attention to accidents, **chance**, what just happens, *flukiness*, **random events**, the way things fall, **unpredictability**, IMPROBABILITY, remote possibility, *the unexpected*, the unforeseen, *the haphazard*, stray thoughts, *the unintentional*, unthinkingly, **INVOLUNTARILY** and **UNWITTINGLY.**

TRANSFORMATION WILL REVEAL ITSELF

EXISTING

YOUR ESSENCE ADRIFT IN THE MATRIX OF LIFE

nothing is unique

everything is unique

TRANS FORM ATION

TO
CHANGE
FORM
SHAPE
COMPOSITION

MANY
THINK
THIS
IS
IMPOSSIBLE

IT
IS
NOT
IT
IS

ORD IN ARY

in western culture people live with tight hearts▼

this is not so in all societies▼

choose▲

looking for difference

we frighten ourselves

by defining others

as other than us

We all are life

SWEETNESS: *what you feel when you are happy about another's existence.*

A CONCEPT IS NOT ≠ AN EXPERIENCE

Believing we have little in common with other species leaves us in contempt of their needs which are the same as our needs

you are not the solid object that you imagine .

you are permeable energy

love *Transcends* apparent limitation

> The transcendental
> intelligence of
> your heart
> is completely
> different from all
> other aspects of
> your intelligence

LOVE is pragmatic

Tolerance is not right
or ethical
or politically correct

Tolerance is healthy

To be intolerant is to be angry or upset in the presence of others who are different from you. When you were in school, you learned that if you measured a large number of anything natural, those numbers would form a normal curve. So to be intolerant is to be upset a great deal of the time. When you are upset, your sympathetic nervous system becomes active and induces stress. In that state love cannot occur. Then we all live in a lesser world.

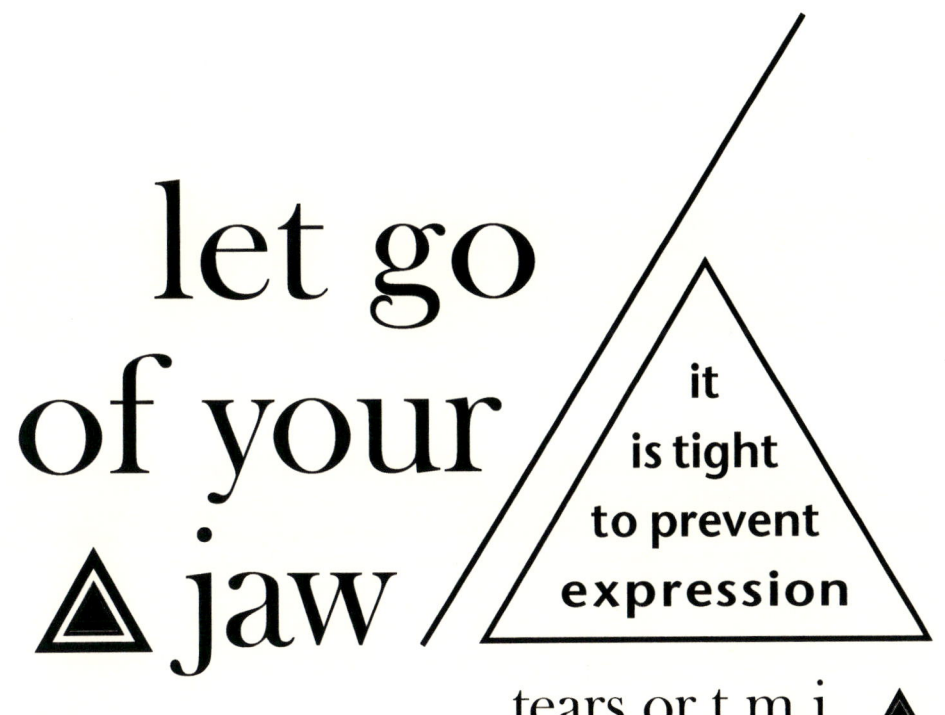

intolerance

intolerance intolerance intolerance intolerance intolerance

fear in the presence of novelty

HEALERS LIVE IN ACCORD WITH THE NATURAL ENVIRONMENT

which is often not in accord with the social environment.

?

If you want to be healthy you must love

The autonomic nervous system controls the involuntary functions of the body. It can make only one of two "choices." If your emotion is anger or fear, the ANS will stimulate your sympathetic nervous system, which prepares you for fight or flight. If your emotion is gentle, the ANS will stimulate the parasympathetic nervous system, which prepares you for relaxation and peace. The former can save your life in true danger, but otherwise creates stress, and then "stress disorders". The latter creates the ideal physical conditions for health and comfort, moment by moment.

One day, in a fit of common sense, the apparent finally became apparent to me. Love is the best we can do.

Dare to know that you are ordinary.

If we imagine that we are different from all that is we will allow ourselves to be murderously destructive

The stars exist for Wonder — they can't be understood — they can't be understood

m | h

life is mysterious

we obscure mystery with habit

HABIT
OBSCURES
THIS
UNIQUE
MOMENT

the **throat** is the center of

CREATIVITY

•

it connects

intelligence

*L*OVE

imagine the all.

that moment is past

the one in the future is only a guess

this leaves us with no past and no future

only reality

hate sickens • love heals

love is the antidote

you know that   you know that also

hate
causes
illness
love
is
the
antidote

hate causes illness

EARTH | HEART

the earth gives you a home | the heart gives you significance

The sum of your choices | Equal your life

pursue
ephemeral & *Become*
percepts

revelation is fleeting

with respect
one views
the other
as equal

not more
not less .

both are
calm

the
moment
passes .

experiential learning potentiates change

didactic learning precipitates thought

information is not knowledge

EVERYTHING IS * LIGHT

To $\dfrac{\text{REALIZE}}{\text{mutability}}$

Quantum Physics

1. ILLNESS RESULTS FROM UNREMITTING CONSISTENCY

2. HEALTH IS AN EXTEMPORANEOUS NOW

1. STILL 2. FLOW

spirituality is not a

SPIRITUALITY IS APPRECIATION OF THE APPARENT

search for 𝕸ysteries

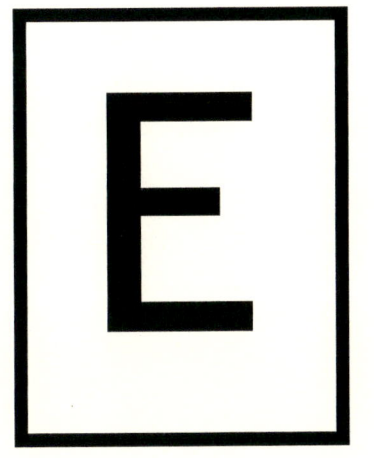 

Experience: | Remember:
see clearly | trompe l'oeil

how do we know? *what do we know?*

forgiving the other
is healing the self

---

it is literally so

a gentle presence is a frictionless context for another's intelligence.
a gentle presence is a frictionless context for another's intelligence.
a gentle presence is a frictionless context for another's intelligence.
a gentle presence is a frictionless context for another's intelligence.
a gentle presence is a frictionless context for another's intelligence.

WE NEVER INTENDED To be the we wHo we are

WE DISCOVER OURSELVES IN EACH MOMENT

LINGER IN THIS MOMENT

NOTHING ELSE EXISTS

Love potentiates

WAITING

as long as
there are
more than
two people
on the earth
we must wait

Wait with an Open Heart

Your existence depends upon nature. Treat your surroundings as if your life depended upon them. It does.

you are not a **THING**

you are a process…

change over time

ordinary
we fear being astonished

so we create ordinary

we all flow with life's energy

anyone can find differences

we all live in the same place

experience your oneness with all life

⎫
relation
connection
correlation
analogy
link
tie
bond
⎭

being human is fine, but never forget, we are merely one species among many

insight

yourself

showing yourself

to yourself

you almost flirting with you

sacred self-revelation
of what you might become

until another insight leads you

imitate — initiate

sleepwalk — stub toe

Conventional Behavior

unthinking repetition of someone else's something other

because we do not perceive nature as our home

WE DO NOT KNOW THAT WE ARE HOME

to not feel at home is in itself, an illness.

so we do not feel at home

FORGIVE because anger corrodes *you*

nature provides the fuel for love

hover in the **PRESENT**

time

the past is *merely* **MEMORY**

reality

the **FUTURE** will be another **now.**

imagine all
imagine one
imagine light
imagine life

imagine the unimaginable

Healing
is
done
with
the
energy
of the
heart

Love heals both healer and patient.

This statement is inconsistent with social belief and medical practice

---

Healing is done with the energy of the heart

tolerate Not knowing

Love is Intelligence

a bold assertion
in a society
that confuses
intelligence
with intellect.

nature is life
you are a part of nature
take very good care of nature

Oindependence *is* XYMORONIC

Human beings are social animals. They cannot live without other people. Humans exist in a living environment composed of many species of plants, animals, and fungi. We depend on one another to exist. We are interdendent.

there is no other place to stand except on the earth

YOU LIVE HERE

problem? failed perception of your physical location

THIS IS YOUR ECOLOGY LESSON

- You are nature.
- Health is consistency with nature.
- Spirituality is experiencing nature.
- Do not turn nature into industrial waste.

the earth is the meeting point of your ego and reality

pollute: to choose to live in your garbage

 You flow with life, so do all animals, plants and fungi. Pollution sickens the flow of life.

Love

Gently defy your culture every day as you discover the experience of love anew

has little place in

our Society

It does not create income !
It is not technological !
It is not fashionable !
It is not scientific !

There is no place for this practice other than in all the moments of our lives.

forgive

reliquish your anger choose love instead

END CEASELESS INTERNAL UPLEASANTNESS

FINISH UNFINISHED EVENTS

Anger, resentment, bitterness, contempt, and grudge-bearing cause displeasure, energy loss, less happiness, and physical disease. Try forgiving.

it will release you from anger and fear

stop internal conversations which haunt you

FORGIVE
FORGIVE

when
LOVING

———

one
neither
gives
nor
takes

———

giving and taking describe commerce
being or doing might describe love

Love heals pain. Love eases despair. Love informs meaninglessness. Love evokes appreciativeness. Love supports gentleness. Love is by its nature kind. Love corrects illness. Love is generous. Love feels good. Love makes us happy.

the moment of love is the reward

IMPORTANT LIST

FEEL THE SENSATIONS OF YOUR HEART
PAY ATTENTION TO NATURE
ENDURE AWE
TOLERATE NOT KNOWING

Our society pays attention to buying and selling. It imagines the living world as assets or objects of scientific inquiry. Do not give up your humanity. Instead do these.

LOVE

is not something you should do.

It is the intelligent choice.

Lay your hand on your chest, put attention to the sensation. Do this a few times a day. The sensations will grow, and begin to engage your heart. You will begin to feel your heart and this will make you happy.

THERE IS NO LOSS IN GIVING
THE HEART KNOWS

the heart does not do double entry bookkeeping

NOW
BE
NOW

Now do now.
Now exist now.
Now be present now.
Now pay attention now.
Now flow now.
Now hover now.
Now unprecedented now.
Now quintessential now.
Now original now.
Now is inherently now.
Now is ontologically now.
Now is your now.
Now is your only now.
Now is your only possibility now.
Now is empirically real now.
Now is the existential absolute.
Now is phenomenology.

LOVE COSTS Ø

Love costs nothing

in this place where a price is affixed to all things and all sevices

Economics of love

Ø

can't save it
can't count it
can't invest it
can only give it away,
bringing joy to your entire existence

The earth
its many forms of life
provide all
that we need

ORDERLINESS OF EXISTENCE

We are absolutely interdependent with all other species

If we destroy
other species
we will be
vulnerable
to disease
and starvation

OBLIVIOUSNESS TO OUTCOME *allows* INSTINCTIVE INTELLIGENCE

brilliant spontaneous & unsocialized creativity

intelligence is vast, intellect is not

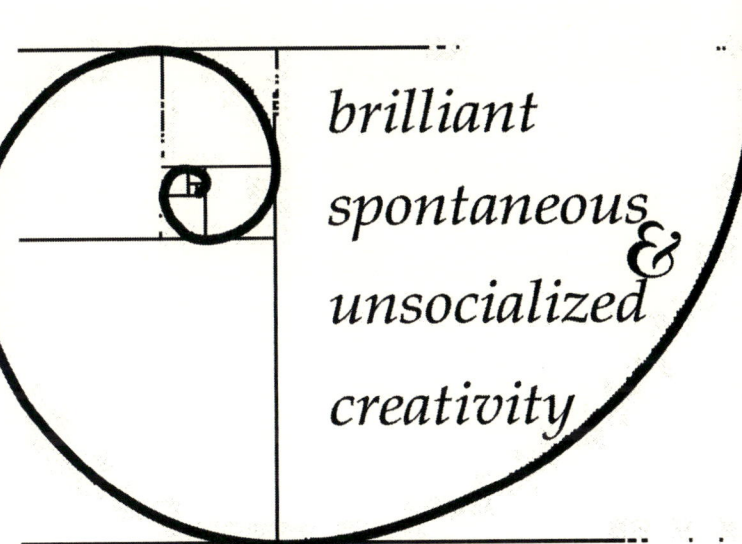

- exchange anger for love changing stress into calm
- anything that feels that unpleasant is not healthy
- it cannot allow you peace
- it cannot make you happy

forgive

Words cannot explain life.